TOP 100 WOMEN IN POWER

CELEBRATING WOMEN'S HISTORY MONTH

WITH YOUR HOSTS

NATOSHA, WENDY, & ANISA

Letter From the Co-Founder

ANISA CRESPO

Welcome to Million Dollar Mom Inc Magazine.
This magazine was created for the woman who knows there is more inside her, more purpose, more power, more impact, and more wealth waiting to be claimed. It was built for the woman who has walked through fire, carried invisible weight, and still chose to rise, even when no one was watching.

Million Dollar Mom Inc was not born from ease. It was born from experience. From loss, rebuilding, faith, resilience, and the unwavering belief that women deserve access to rooms, resources, and representation that reflect their true value. I know what it feels like to come from scarcity, to navigate grief, addiction, fear, and financial hardship, and still hear a quiet inner voice whisper, this is not the end of your story. This magazine is a response to that voice.

We created this platform to amplify women who are building something real. Not just businesses, but legacies. Women who are willing to be visible, even when it feels uncomfortable. Women who understand that visibility is not vanity, it is responsibility. When one woman is seen, another finds permission.

Inside these pages, you will find stories that are raw, honest, and powerful. You will find expertise earned through experience, not just theory. You will find women who have dared to believe that motherhood and ambition are not opposites, but partners. Million Dollar Mom Inc is more than a magazine. It is a movement rooted in visibility, influence, and impact. Every feature, every article, every cover is intentional. We are building an ecosystem where women are not only showcased, but supported. Where stories do not disappear after publication, but continue to live through global distribution, media amplification, and real opportunity.

My hope is that as you read these pages, you see yourself reflected somewhere inside. Maybe in a story that feels familiar. Maybe in a dream you have been afraid to say out loud. Maybe in a version of you that is ready to step forward.
You belong here.

Thank you for being part of this community, whether you are a reader, a contributor, or a woman standing on the edge of her next chapter. This magazine exists because of women like you.

With faith, gratitude, and belief in what is possible,
Anisa Crespo
Co-Founder, Million Dollar Mom Inc

Letter From the Co-Founder

NATOSHA NAVARRO

Welcome to Million Dollar Mom Inc Magazine.
If you are holding this magazine, there is a reason. You are not here by accident. You are here because something inside you knows that growth requires expansion, and expansion requires courage.

As a mom, a wife, and a serial entrepreneur, I understand the pull of ambition alongside the demands of family. I understand what it means to build businesses while raising children, navigating seasons of uncertainty, and constantly reinventing yourself as life evolves. I have worked across multiple industries, coached hundreds of women, and watched one truth remain consistent, women thrive when they are supported, seen, and strategically guided.

This magazine was created to be that support. Million Dollar Mom Inc is a space where women are allowed to want more without guilt. More income. More freedom. More fulfillment. More alignment. It is a place where ambition is honored, not minimized, and where strategy and belief walk hand in hand.

Inside these pages, you will meet women who have taken risks, pivoted paths, and trusted themselves even when the outcome was uncertain. You will see stories that reflect the reality of entrepreneurship, the wins, the lessons, and the resilience required to keep going.

Visibility matters. When women share their stories and expertise, they create ripple effects far beyond themselves. They inspire action, spark confidence, and shift what feels possible for the next woman watching. This magazine exists to create those ripple effects on a global scale.

As a co-founder, my commitment is to ensure that Million Dollar Mom Inc remains rooted in value, integrity, and impact. We are not here to chase trends. We are here to build something lasting. Something that supports women in becoming financially empowered, strategically sound, and deeply confident in their ability to lead.
I hope this magazine challenges you to think bigger, trust deeper, and take the next step toward the life and business you desire. Whether that step is visibility, growth, or simply believing in yourself a little more than you did yesterday, it matters.
Thank you for being part of this community and for contributing to a future where women rise together.

With purpose and possibility,
Natosha Navarro
Co-Founder, Million Dollar Mom Inc

Letter From the Co-Founder

WENDY AIMEE PORTER

Welcome to Million Dollar Mom Inc Magazine.

This magazine represents more than success stories. It represents courage. The courage to be seen. The courage to speak your truth. The courage to step into rooms that once felt inaccessible.

Throughout my journey as an entrepreneur, mentor, and leader, I have witnessed firsthand what happens when women claim their voice and visibility. When women stop shrinking to fit expectations and start expanding into their purpose, everything changes. Not just for them, but for the communities they serve.

Million Dollar Mom Inc was created to hold space for that expansion.

This platform exists to honor women who are building meaningful businesses while navigating real lives. Women who are balancing vision with responsibility, ambition with heart, and leadership with authenticity. Women who understand that wealth is not just financial, but relational, emotional, and generational.

Inside this magazine, you will find stories that remind you that you are not alone. That doubt is part of growth. That clarity often comes after action. And that your voice has value, even if you are still becoming the woman you envision.

Visibility is powerful. When women are visible, they are remembered. When they are remembered, opportunities follow. This magazine was designed to not only showcase women, but to elevate them through intentional exposure, strategic amplification, and global reach.

As a co-founder, my role is rooted in championing women to step fully into who they are becoming. To trust their intuition. To honor their experiences. To lead with confidence and compassion. Million Dollar Mom Inc is a reflection of what happens when women support women without competition, comparison, or limitation.
My hope is that these pages leave you inspired, affirmed, and ready to take bold action in your life and business. Whatever season you are in, know that your story matters, and your presence here is meaningful. Thank you for being part of this movement and for helping shape a future where women are visible, influential, and impactful.

With belief in your brilliance,
Wendy Aimee Porter
Co-Founder, Million Dollar Mom Inc

MILLION DOLLAR
Mom Inc Magazine

TABLE OF CONTENTS

Front Cover Feature: Wanda Santos-Haynes From Roommates to Romance.....08

Back Cover Feature: From Classroom to Crusade: How Amy Benjamin Moore Is Rewriting the Menopause Playbook.....17

From Survival to Legacy: The Purpose-Driven Rise of Jay Kay.....24

Building Beyond Burnout: How Kym Brake Turned Tax Strategy Into a Life-First Business Model for Entrepreneurs.....31

MARCH 2026 EDITION

MILLION DOLLAR

Mom Inc Magazine

TABLE OF CONTENTS

When Enough is Enough by Angela Devani....................38

Becoming the Liminal Woman: The Practice of Self-Governance in the In-Between Times by Allie Billings....................43

When Soundbites Weren't Enough: The Birth and Vision of WSOS: Scripture Over Soundbites by Kelly Parker....................48

Hot Flashes & Cold Truths: A No-Nonsense Guide to Menopause Because if we don't laugh, we'll cry... and then forget why we were crying by Amy Benjamin Moore....................53

COVER FEATURE

From Roommates to Romance

How Wanda Santos-Haynes is Redefining Love, Power, and Intimacy for High-Achieving Women

From Roommates to Romance

with Wanda Santos-Haynes

THE SILENT CRISIS INSIDE SUCCESSFUL RELATIONSHIPS

On the outside, everything looks beautiful. The career is thriving. The home is well-appointed. The calendar is full. The life that many women once dreamed of has been built through discipline, resilience, and relentless self-belief. Yet behind closed doors, something feels painfully absent. The intimacy is quiet. The conversations are logistical. The connection that once felt alive now feels distant, dutiful, or flat.

This is the silent crisis Wanda Santos-Haynes has dedicated her life to addressing.

As a relationship and intimacy expert and PhD student in clinical sexology, Wanda works with high-achieving women and couples who appear successful by every external metric, yet feel profoundly lonely in their most intimate relationships. They are not broken. They are not failing. They are operating from nervous systems trained for survival rather than connection.

Wanda's work sits at the intersection of neuroscience, attachment theory, trauma-informed healing, and embodied leadership. Her clients are often powerful women who have mastered strategy, performance, and independence, but were never taught how to feel safe enough to soften, receive, and desire.

What makes Wanda's approach distinctive is that she does not treat intimacy as a surface-level communication problem. She understands it as a biological, emotional, and relational system shaped by early experiences, unprocessed trauma, cultural conditioning, and the demands placed on modern women to be everything to everyone.

In her practice, Wanda often names the moment couples stop feeling like lovers and start feeling like roommates. It is rarely sudden. It happens slowly, through missed bids for connection, chronic stress, unresolved resentment, and nervous systems locked in protection. Desire fades not because love disappears, but because safety, polarity, and emotional attunement erode.

Rather than offering quick fixes or performative intimacy tips, Wanda guides her clients through deep pattern recognition. She helps them understand how childhood attachment wounds, trauma bonds, and survival strategies show up in adult partnerships. She teaches them how power dynamics, money, and emotional labor quietly shape attraction and trust.

At the core of her philosophy is a radical truth. Love is not sustained by grand gestures. It is grown in micro-moments. In the tone of a voice. In the way conflict is navigated. In whether a nervous system feels seen or threatened.

Wanda's message is clear. Secure, passionate love is not about luck. It is about healing the body, understanding relational patterns, and choosing connection daily.

FROM CLINICAL TRAINING TO LIVED WISDOM

Wanda Santos-Haynes did not arrive at her work through theory alone. Her authority is grounded in both rigorous clinical training and deeply lived experience. With more than two decades in coaching, counseling, and education, she has witnessed how unhealed trauma quietly infiltrates love, money, identity, and leadership.

A defining moment in Wanda's journey came through profound personal loss. In the midst of grief, she observed how quickly stress, fear, and unresolved wounds can fracture even the most committed relationships. She saw how emotional disconnection does not stem from a lack of love, but from nervous systems overwhelmed by survival.
That moment reshaped her path.

Rather than compartmentalizing her pain, Wanda chose integration. She committed to blending neuroscience, attachment theory, and embodied healing with the wisdom that only lived experience can offer. Her work became less about fixing people and more about teaching them how to feel safe enough to be fully present with one another.

As a PhD student in clinical sexology, Wanda brings academic rigor to a space often dominated by oversimplified advice. She understands intimacy as a multidimensional experience involving the brain, the body, emotional memory, and relational dynamics. Her frameworks address not only desire and communication, but also trauma responses, nervous system regulation, and power balance.

This depth has made her a sought-after speaker, mentor, and educator. Clients are drawn to her rare ability to hold complexity without judgment. She speaks to high-achieving women in a language they trust, one that honors both strength and vulnerability.

Wanda's work also challenges a common cultural narrative. Many women are taught that independence and self-sufficiency are the ultimate goals. While these qualities are powerful, Wanda highlights the cost when independence becomes armor rather than choice. When strength replaces softness. When success replaces intimacy.

Her approach does not ask women to shrink or abandon their ambition. Instead, it invites them to expand their capacity for connection without sacrificing power. She teaches that true partnership is not about managing a partner, but about co-regulating, co-creating, and building relational safety together.

This philosophy is not theoretical. Wanda lives it. She speaks openly about the pride she takes in building a thriving practice while maintaining a deeply connected, loving marriage. For her, success is not measured solely in professional milestones, but in the quality of presence shared at home.

WHY STRONG WOMEN FEEL LONELY IN LOVE

One of the most common questions Wanda encounters is deceptively simple. Why do so many high-achieving women feel lonely in their relationships despite having everything they worked for?

The answer lies in patterning.

Many successful women learned early that safety came from competence. They became problem-solvers, caretakers, and leaders. Over time, these survival strategies turned into identity. While they created professional success, they often suppressed needs, emotions, and vulnerability in intimate spaces.

Wanda explains that when a woman's nervous system is accustomed to control and responsibility, intimacy can feel unsafe. Desire requires presence, receptivity, and emotional risk. If the body associates closeness with threat or disappointment, it will shut down attraction to protect itself.

This is where many couples become stuck in roommate dynamics. Emotional labor becomes one-sided. Sexual desire fades. Communication becomes transactional. Resentment quietly builds.

Wanda's work reframes these patterns without blame. She teaches that attraction is not a moral failing. It is a physiological response. When the nervous system feels overwhelmed, unseen, or burdened, desire naturally retreats.

Money and power further complicate this dynamic. In relationships where women out-earn or emotionally manage their partners, polarity can collapse. Wanda addresses this with nuance, helping couples renegotiate roles without reinforcing outdated gender scripts.

Central to her methodology is nervous system regulation. When both partners learn how to recognize their stress responses, soothe emotional reactivity, and create safety during conflict, intimacy begins to return organically.

Wanda emphasizes that rebuilding passion does not start in the bedroom. It starts in the nervous system. In how partners listen. In how they repair after rupture. In whether both feel emotionally held rather than managed.

Her clients often experience a profound shift when they realize intimacy is not something to perform. It is something to feel.

THE ROOMMATE SYNDROME AND THE PATH BACK TO DESIRE

Wanda Santos-Haynes is widely known for her work around what she calls the roommate dynamic. It is a state many couples normalize without realizing its long-term impact. Shared responsibilities replace shared intimacy. Conversations revolve around logistics. Touch becomes functional or disappears altogether.

Wanda's Roommate to Romance framework helps individuals and couples identify how they arrived there and how to consciously choose something different.

She begins by addressing emotional safety. Without safety, desire cannot thrive. Many couples attempt to reignite passion without addressing resentment, emotional disconnection, or unresolved conflict. Wanda teaches that the nervous system will not allow intimacy where there is unspoken tension.

Her process includes understanding attachment styles, trauma bonds, and childhood conditioning. Clients learn how early experiences shape adult expectations of love, conflict, and closeness. This awareness alone can dissolve years of self-blame.

Wanda also addresses polarity. Desire thrives on difference, presence, and energetic balance. When partners fall into parent-child or manager-managed roles, attraction naturally declines. Restoring polarity requires conscious shifts in communication, responsibility, and emotional labor.

Importantly, Wanda's work honors timing. She reassures couples that passion can be rebuilt even after years of disconnection. The body remembers safety. The heart remembers desire.

Through programs like Breaking the Pattern and The Love He Feels Again, Wanda offers structured pathways for healing. These experiences guide clients through nervous system regulation, communication repair, and embodied reconnection.

What emerges is not a return to who they once were, but the creation of a new relational identity grounded in choice, awareness, and mutual respect.

LOVE, MONEY, AND FEMININE LEADERSHIP

One of the most groundbreaking aspects of Wanda's work is her willingness to explore the intersection of love, money, and identity. She understands that financial power often mirrors emotional power within relationships.

Many women were never taught how to hold wealth and intimacy simultaneously. Success can trigger guilt, resentment, or imbalance if unexamined. Wanda helps couples navigate these conversations with honesty and compassion.

She teaches that financial dynamics are not just logistical. They are emotional. They activate deep beliefs about worth, safety, and control. When addressed consciously, they can strengthen rather than fracture connection.

Wanda also speaks passionately about feminine leadership. True leadership, in her view, includes emotional literacy, embodiment, and relational intelligence. It is not about dominance or submission, but about presence and attunement.

As Wanda expands into global thought leadership, she is committed to elevating relational literacy worldwide. Through education, media, and high-touch coaching, she is redefining what it means to succeed both professionally and personally.

The Invitation to *Thrive*

At the heart of Wanda Santos-Haynes' message is an invitation. To stop settling. To stop surviving. To stop believing that love fades with time.

She reminds her audience that intimacy is not accidental. It is cultivated through awareness, nervous system healing, and daily choice. Secure, passionate love is available to those willing to understand themselves deeply and show up intentionally.

Wanda's legacy is not only in the couples she helps heal, but in the cultural shift she champions. One where success and intimacy coexist. Where power and softness are not opposites. Where love is treated as a living system deserving of care.

Her work stands as a reminder that the most influential women do not just build empires. They build relationships that nourish them from the inside out.

Connect With Wanda Santos-Haynes

wandasantoshaynes.com

Social Media

Wanda Santos-Haynes
https://www.facebook.com/wanda.santos.3597

@wandasantos_haynes
https://www.instagram.com/wandasantos_haynes/

@wandasantos_haynes
https://www.tiktok.com/@wandasantos_haynes

FEATURED OFFERS

LEARN MORE ON WANDASANTOSHAYNES.COM

Breaking the *Pattern*

Breaking the Pattern is a transformational experience designed to help individuals identify and heal unconscious attachment wounds, trauma bonds, and relationship cycles that keep them stuck in unfulfilling or unhealthy dynamics. This program guides participants through deep pattern recognition, nervous system regulation, and emotional healing so they can stop repeating the past and consciously choose secure, emotionally available love.

The Love He Feels Again

The Love He Feels Again is a relationship restoration experience for women and couples who feel emotionally distant, disconnected, or stuck in roommate dynamics. This program focuses on rebuilding emotional safety, attraction, and intimacy by shifting communication patterns, regulating the nervous system, and restoring polarity. The result is a natural return of love, desire, and connection without forcing change or performing intimacy.

From Classroom to Crusade

How **Amy Benjamin Moore** Is Rewriting the Menopause Playbook

Amy Benjamin Moore spent three decades teaching. She never imagined her most important lesson would come from her own body. And that millions of women would need to hear it.

The clues started appearing in her mid-forties. Shoulder pain. Heart palpitations. Brain fog that made her question her own competence. Like most high-achieving women, Amy treated each symptom as a separate problem to solve. She went to an orthopedic doctor for what she assumed was a painting injury. Frozen shoulder, he diagnosed. "What caused it?" she asked, certain it was connected to the ceiling she'd painted weeks before.

"We don't know why," he told her. "But we do know it's prevalent in women ages 45 to 55."

The age range hung in the air between them.

Amy didn't make the connection. Neither did he.

The heart palpitations sent her to a cardiologist. You're fine, she was told. The fatigue, the mood shifts, the inexplicable changes, each became its own mystery. She was doing what so many capable women do: investigating symptoms individually, never seeing the pattern.

"I was solving problems in isolation," Amy says now. "I never thought to ask: what do all of these have in common? And honestly, even if I had asked, I wouldn't have known the answer. Nobody taught me what perimenopause looked like."

It wasn't until later, after months of research, after stumbling across information that should have been common knowledge, that the pieces finally clicked into place. Frozen shoulder. Heart palpitations. Brain fog. Mood changes. Every single symptom she'd been chasing? Perimenopause.

The realization was clarifying. And infuriating.

"I'm educated. I'm resourceful. I spent 31 years in schools," Amy reflects. "And I was completely in the dark. If I didn't know, how many other women were navigating this blind?"
More importantly, how many would continue to, unless someone broke the silence?

THE PIVOT

That question became the catalyst for what would become Dream, Build, & Succeed, LLC. A complete career reinvention built on solving a problem Amy had lived with.

After three decades as an educator, Amy made the decision that would redefine her legacy. She became a GGS-Certified Menopause Coaching Specialist. Not to help women "cope" with menopause. To educate them. To arm them with the information she'd had to hunt down herself.

"I refused to let my daughters and nieces go through what I went through," she says. "This generational silence ends with us."

It's a bold mission. And Amy approached it the way any entrepreneur would: by building infrastructure.

She created the Menopause Mastery Toolkit app, a comprehensive resource that provides women with the education and solutions no one else offers. Then the Menopause Symptom Tracker app, so women could finally see patterns instead of isolated incidents. She built a coaching practice. A social media presence that blends education with humor and honesty. A community of women who'd spent too long thinking they were alone.

And in 2026, her debut book releases: Hot Flashes & Cold Truths: A No-Nonsense Guide to Menopause (Because If We Don't Laugh, We'll Cry… and Then Forget Why We Were Crying).

The title alone signals Amy's approach: unflinching, educational, and refreshingly human.

BUILDING ON WHAT WAS BROKEN

What makes Amy's work resonate isn't just the information. It's the mission behind it. She's not building a business. She's breaking a generational pattern.

"There are conversations I wish I could have with my mother," Amy wrote recently in her upcoming article for this magazine. "Menopause is one of them. Not because she's unwilling, but because it was never part of her vocabulary. The silence was already set before either of us knew we needed the words."

That silence shaped Amy's perimenopause experience. It's what sent her to specialists who treated symptoms without context. It's why she spent months doubting her competence rather than understanding her biology.

And it's exactly what she's dismantling, one conversation, one app download, and one coaching session at a time.

Her clients are high-achieving women who've spent careers leading teams, building businesses, and solving complex problems. Women who suddenly found themselves questioning everything because no one had prepared them for this transition.

"These are capable, brilliant women," Amy says. "They don't need to be coddled. They need information. They need context. They need to know they're not failing. They're just navigating a biological shift that nobody bothered to explain."

THE EMPIRE *is* EDUCATION

Amy's business model is unconventional in its simplicity: give women what the medical system, their mothers, and society at large failed to provide. Preparation. Education. Permission to take up space during midlife instead of shrinking from it.

Her "Menopause Minute" newsletter reaches her audience weekly. Her social media content connects with women navigating the same questions she once had. Her apps provide practical tools. Her coaching offers a strategy; her book is the manual you never received; and her course is the roadmap to reclaiming yourself.

But the through-line in everything Amy builds? Sustainable self-care without apology.

"We've been conditioned to push through," she explains. "To perform through exhaustion. To apologize for needing support. I'm teaching women that sustainable leadership means honoring your biology, not fighting it."

It's a message that resonates particularly now, as more women in leadership speak openly about menopause in the workplace. As employers begin recognizing midlife support as a retention strategy. As the conversation shifts from whispered thoughts to public advocacy.

Amy is part of that shift. And she's documenting it, teaching through it, building businesses around it.

LEGACY WORK

When asked what success looks like, Amy doesn't talk about revenue or reach. She talks about her daughter. Her nieces. The next generation of women who won't have to play detective with their own bodies.

"I want them to enter perimenopause with a roadmap," she says. "I want them to recognize symptoms immediately. I want them to advocate for themselves with doctors who actually understand hormone science. I want them to know this is normal, manageable, and not something to endure in silence."

That's the empire Amy is building. Not just measured in dollars, but also in generational impact.

She built a business by solving the problem she lived. Now she's ensuring her clients, her daughter, and the next generation won't inherit the same silence she did.

After 31 years of teaching, Amy Benjamin Moore is teaching one of the lessons that matters most.

And this time, millions of women are listenin

Connect With Amy Benjamin Moore

https://amybenjaminmoore.com

Social Media

Amy Benjamin Moore
https://www.facebook.com/amy.benjaminmoore

@amybenjaminmoore
https://www.instagram.com/amybenjaminmoore/

Amy Benjamin Moore
https://www.linkedin.com/in/amy-benjamin-moore-315288393/

YOUR MENOPAUSE SURVIVAL GUIDE

Menopause Doesn't Have to Be a Mystery!
Discover the guide that's helping women embrace this phase with knowledge and strength.

DOWNLOAD HERE: survival.amybenjaminmoore.com

Meet the women behind the network

NATOSHA NAVARRO

Co-Founder, Visionary, Executive Producer

Natosha Navarro is a visionary entrepreneur, executive producer, and media architect with a bold mission: to build platforms where women are seen, heard, and remembered.

A former Air Force veteran turned six-figure digital marketing strategist, Natosha scaled her own business from the ground up before co-founding Million Dollar Media Group to create something bigger than a brand — a movement.

With a gift for positioning, proximity, and powerful rooms, Natosha leads the strategic direction of the network, curating high-level opportunities across television, podcasting, live events, and global streaming platforms.

WENDY AIMEE PORTER

Co-Founder, Media Strategist, Executive Producer

Wendy Aimee Porter is a respected media producer and founder known for spotlighting powerful women through high-level events and recognition platforms.

As a co-founder of Million Dollar Media Group, Wendy brings years of experience producing premium media experiences, red carpet events, and authority-building platforms for female leaders.

Her commitment to visibility, credibility, and curated excellence strengthens the network's reach and influence, helping create powerful stages where women are celebrated, recognized, and elevated.

ANISA CRESPO

Co-Founder, Brand Strategist, Executive Producer

Anisa Crespo is a powerhouse brand strategist and co-creator of Million Dollar Media Group. With a background in corporate leadership and high-level operations, Anisa brings precision, structure, and scale to the vision.

She specializes in helping women refine their positioning, elevate their messaging, and expand their impact through media.

Anisa is passionate about collaboration over competition and believes that when women build together, they build stronger. Inside the network, she plays a key role in brand development, show creation, and ensuring every opportunity aligns with excellence, strategy, and long-term growth.

Hit play on Roku, Apple TV, or Fire TV today!

WATCH NOW

From Survival to Legacy: The Purpose-Driven Rise of Jay Kay

The Purpose-Driven Rise of Jay Kay

FROM SURVIVAL MODE TO PURPOSE MODE

Jay Kay's journey is not one defined by ease, but by intention. Like many women who carry both vision and responsibility, she spent years navigating life in survival mode. Responsibilities were heavy, transitions were painful, and uncertainty became a constant companion. Yet it was within that pressure that clarity emerged.

There came a season when Jay Kay recognized that simply enduring was no longer enough. Survival had kept her standing, but it was not allowing her to expand. In that moment of reckoning, she made a decision that would redefine everything that followed. She chose to rebuild her life deliberately, not from fear, but from purpose.
That choice became the foundation of her work today.

Jay Kay often speaks about the difference between reacting to life and responding to it. Survival mode reacts. Purpose mode responds with intention, strategy, and vision. The shift did not remove hardship overnight, but it changed how she showed up. She began to release what no longer served her and create space for who she was becoming.

One of her most resonant beliefs was born in that season: isolation, when used intentionally, can become elevation. What felt like loss or separation was actually preparation. With fewer distractions, her focus sharpened. Her voice grew stronger. Her calling became undeniable.

Today, Jay Kay uses that lived experience as a bridge for others. Her story resonates because it is not aspirational fantasy, it is lived truth. She reminds audiences that no matter how long you have been surviving, you can choose differently. You can rebuild. You can rise. And you can step into a purpose that honors both where you have been and where you are going.

WEARING MANY WIGS AND OWNING EVERY ONE

Jay Kay is widely known for embracing the truth that most people live multifaceted lives. Entrepreneur, leader, mentor, speaker, creator, visionary. Instead of asking people to choose one identity, she invites them to own them all.

This philosophy came to life through The Many Wigs Podcast, a platform she created to highlight the many roles people carry and the complexity behind success. The podcast is not about perfection or polished personas. It is about authenticity, resilience, and the courage to show up fully as yourself, even while evolving.

Through powerful conversations, Jay Kay creates space for entrepreneurs and leaders to share their stories of reinvention. She normalizes the reality that growth often requires shedding old versions of ourselves and stepping into new ones before we feel fully ready.

Beyond media, Jay Kay's impact is deeply rooted in wealth building and stability. With more than two decades in real estate, along with work in credit restoration and financial education, she has helped individuals and families take tangible steps toward homeownership and generational wealth. Her approach is practical, accessible, and grounded in empowerment rather than intimidation.

She is also the co-founder of Ascend Security, a company created from her commitment to building safer communities, and the co-creator of Le'Elegance, a luxury fragrance brand that reflects confidence, identity, and elevation.

Across every venture, one thing remains consistent. Jay Kay builds businesses that serve people. Her work is not about titles or trends. It is about equipping others with tools, confidence, and clarity so they can rise personally, professionally, and financially.

TURNING PAIN INTO PURPOSE AND POWER

What sets Jay Kay apart is not just what she has built, but how she built it. Her reputation is rooted in transformation. She is known for turning pain into purpose and teaching others how to do the same.

Her storytelling is raw yet refined. She does not shy away from difficult seasons, but she also does not glorify struggle. Instead, she reframes adversity as a teacher. Each challenge carried a lesson. Each setback revealed strength. Each ending created space for a new beginning.

As a speaker and thought leader, Jay Kay's message is clear. You do not have to stay in survival mode. No matter what your past holds, you have the power to rebuild your life with intention. Purpose is not reserved for those with perfect beginnings. It is claimed by those willing to rise after disruption.

She encourages audiences to recognize when it is time to release. Release old narratives. Release environments that no longer align. Release versions of themselves that were created solely to survive. Growth, she teaches, requires honesty and courage.

Through her platforms, Jay Kay has become a trusted voice for those navigating transition. Entrepreneurs, parents, leaders, and everyday individuals see themselves in her story because it reflects their own. She makes transformation feel possible, not overwhelming.

Her work reminds us that legacy is not built overnight. It is built through consistent choices, aligned action, and the willingness to lead from experience rather than perfection.

STEPPING INTO LEGACY AND VISIBILITY

Today, Jay Kay is in a season of expansion. Her leadership is evolving, her visibility is growing, and her vision is larger than ever. She is stepping fully into her role as a mentor, guide, and legacy builder.

She continues to expand her voice through speaking, media, and live platforms, including the evolution of The Many Wigs Podcast into The Many Wigs Talk Show. This next chapter represents growth, reach, and deeper impact. It is a reflection of her commitment to meet people where they are and guide them toward where they are meant to be.

Professionally, she remains anchored in real estate, credit education, community safety through Ascend Security, and the development of Le'Elegance. Each venture is part of a larger ecosystem designed to support stability, confidence, and long-term wealth.

What Jay Kay is most proud of is not just what she has built, but who she has become in the process. A woman who leads from experience. A woman who chooses intention over fear. A woman who understands that visibility is not about being seen for recognition, but being seen so others know what is possible.

Her message to audiences is simple yet powerful. You are not defined by your circumstances. You can rebuild your life. You can rise into purpose. And you can create a legacy that extends far beyond you.

Jay Kay stands as a reminder that when women step into alignment, visibility, and purpose, they do not just change their own lives. They change generations.

WhoIsJayKay.Com & **TheManyWigsPodcast.VIP** & **LeElegance.Com**

Connect on Socials

WhoIsJayKay
https://www.instagram.com/WhoIsJayKay/

TheManyWigsPodcast
https://www.instagram.com/TheManyWigsPodcast/

LeElegance.Co
https://www.instagram.com/LeElegance.Co/

ARE YOU A PODCAST CREATOR READY TO EXPAND YOUR LISTENER BASE AND REACH NEW AUDIENCES AROUND THE WORLD?

The Podcast Creator Channel on Million Dollar Network is a **curated media space** designed to **amplify powerful voices** through *professionally showcased podcasts* **streamed across major platforms including Roku TV, Apple TV, Amazon Fire, and more.**

MDN positions your show inside a **global network built for visibility, credibility, and growth.**

Your podcast becomes part of a **powerful lineup of women-led content** created to **educate, inspire, and influence audiences worldwide.**

A **BIGGER** PLATFORM.

A **GLOBAL** AUDIENCE.

A **NEW LEVEL** OF VISIBILITY.

The **Podcast Creator Channel** was built for hosts who are ready to **expand their reach beyond traditional podcast platforms** and step into the world of **streaming media distribution.**

Inside the Million Dollar Network ecosystem, your podcast is **professionally showcased** alongside an **elite network of creators** who are shaping conversations, building influence, and reaching audiences on a global scale.

We are **currently accepting applications from podcast hosts** who are ready to **elevate their brand and expand their audience** through global streaming exposure.

If you have a podcast — or a powerful message ready to be shared — **this is your opportunity to step onto a larger stage.**

I'M READY FOR MY PODCAST TO BE ON TV!

MILLION DOLLAR NETWORK

Building Beyond Burnout

How **Kym Brake** Turned Tax Strategy Into a Life-First Business Model for Entrepreneurs

HOW NECESSITY BECAME THE FOUNDATION OF A MODERN TAX FIRM

Some businesses are born from passion. Others are born from necessity. For Kym Brake, it was both.

Long before remote work became mainstream, Kym was building a fully virtual tax practice out of survival and responsibility. As a young single mother navigating hospital stays, therapy appointments, and the realities of special-needs parenting, flexibility was not optional.

It was essential. What began as bookkeeping work to create stability slowly evolved into something far bigger.

Kym's natural ability to organize, explain, and simplify complex financial concepts became the backbone of her growing client base. As demand increased, so did her commitment to mastery. She pursued advanced education, earning an LL.M. in Tax Law, and spent years working closely under a former IRS auditor and Enrolled Agent.

That experience gave her an insider-level understanding of compliance, audits, and the gaps where misinformation often puts business owners at risk.

OC Tax Brake was built to close those gaps.

Today, the firm serves more than 700 clients nationwide, specializing in proactive tax planning, entity structuring, and education-driven strategies designed to help entrepreneurs keep more of what they earn legally and sustainably. But what truly sets Kym apart is her approach. She does not believe taxes should feel secretive, intimidating, or transactional. She believes they should feel strategic, empowering, and rooted in real life.

Every system, service, and strategy within OC Tax Brake reflects that belief. It is not just a tax firm. It is a resource for business owners who want clarity instead of confusion and confidence instead of fear.

REDEFINING TAX STRATEGY THROUGH EDUCATION AND INTEGRITY

In an industry often filled with conflicting advice and risky shortcuts, Kym Brake has become known for something rare: clarity with integrity.

Kym's reputation has been built on her ability to translate complex tax law into practical, audit-proof strategies entrepreneurs can actually understand.

She is unapologetic about calling out misinformation in the tax space, especially when it puts business owners at risk under the guise of "write-offs" and loopholes that are neither compliant nor sustainable.

Education is at the heart of everything she does.

Rather than positioning herself as a gatekeeper of knowledge, Kym believes empowered clients make better decisions. OC Tax Brake focuses on proactive planning, helping clients understand entity structures, deductions, and long-term strategy before problems arise. This forward-thinking approach allows business owners to stop reacting to tax season and start using taxes as a tool for growth and protection.

Kym is especially passionate about helping entrepreneurs move from fear to confidence. Many of her clients come in overwhelmed, unsure of what applies to them, and anxious about audits or mistakes. Through education-driven systems and transparent communication, she helps them regain control and understand how to operate strategically without crossing lines.

Her work goes beyond numbers. It's about trust. It's about sustainability. And it's about ensuring business owners are not building success on unstable foundations.

By combining technical expertise with real-life application, Kym has reshaped how her clients experience taxes. What once felt intimidating becomes manageable. What felt confusing becomes clear. And what felt risky becomes intentional.

WHEN BUSINESS BECAME ABOUT PROTECTION, NOT JUST GROWTH

There are moments in life that permanently shift perspective. For Kym Brake, that moment came when her daughter nearly lost her life.

In the face of that reality, time, security, and success took on entirely new meaning. Growth for growth's sake was no longer enough. A business dependent solely on client hours and constant availability was no longer sustainable. Kym realized that if her business was going to truly support her family, it needed to evolve.

That realization led to a pivotal shift.

Kym began intentionally building scalable education products, courses, and systems that could create income beyond one-on-one client work. This was not about stepping away from service. It was about designing a business that could fund full-time care, provide flexibility, and allow her to be fully present where she was needed most.

For Kym, sustainability became non-negotiable.

This transition required courage, strategy, and a willingness to pivot long-standing systems. It also required releasing guilt around designing a business that supported her real life instead of sacrificing it. Building education-based products was no longer optional. It was essential for protection, stability, and longevity.

That chapter reshaped how she approached leadership, growth, and success. Her business became a vehicle not just for income, but for resilience. Every decision moving forward was guided by intention, urgency, and heart.

t was in this season that Kym fully stepped into her role as both strategist and educator, creating impact far beyond individual client files.

REDEFINING IDENTITY, RESILIENCE, AND WHAT COMES NEXT

For more than two decades, Kym Brake's identity was rooted in caregiving, responsibility, and survival. She gave everything she had to being a mother and protector, often putting her own needs last. Now, at 43, she finds herself in the most transformative chapter yet.

For the first time, Kym is intentionally focusing on herself.

This season is not about having all the answers. It is about self-discovery, self-trust, and giving herself permission to explore who she is beyond obligation. She is learning what brings her joy, what she no longer wants to carry, and how to lead a life that honors ambition alongside rest, fulfillment, and self-love.

Professionally, she is most proud of never giving up. Of pivoting when necessary. Of expanding beyond tax preparation into education, strategy, and impact. And most importantly, of finding and using her voice.

If there is one takeaway Kym hopes others receive from her journey, it is resilience. Not the performative kind, but the quiet, relentless determination to keep going even when it would be easier to stop.

Today, Kym continues to build with intention, integrity, and heart. Her work empowers entrepreneurs to protect what they are building, and her story reminds women that success does not require self-sacrifice. It requires alignment.

And this chapter is only just beginning.

Connect with Kym

https://www.facebook.com/octaxbrake

https://www.instagram.com/octaxbrake/

ICONIC AF

Are you building something iconic?

APPLY TO BE A GUEST ON ICONIC AF

As we celebrated our 100th episode in December 2025 and step into this next season, we are intentionally curating conversations with women who are building bold businesses, creating meaningful impact, and leading with purpose. This next chapter of the podcast is focused on real strategy, visibility, leadership, energetics, and the lived experience of entrepreneurship as a woman.

Our goal is to feature women who are in the arena. Women who are actively building, growing, evolving, and willing to share the real lessons behind the journey.

This application helps us ensure alignment and maintain the depth, caliber, and integrity of the conversations we are creating.

If you are a woman who is building something meaningful and has insights, experiences, or perspectives that could inspire and empower other women, we would love to learn more about you.

Share your story. Share your strategy. Share your impact.

Apply to be featured on Iconic AF and join a network of women who are shaping the next era of leadership and influence.

APPLY NOW

Media Mogul

TURN YOUR **MESSAGE** INTO A TV TV SHOW

What if **your podcast**… **your expertise**… or **your voice** became a **television-style show** seen by **audiences around the world?**

Media Mogul is a **membership** created by Wendy Aimee Porter, Anisa Crespo, and Natosha Navarro ***designed to help women transform their message into professionally produced shows*** broadcast across the **Million Dollar Network**.

Inside Media Mogul, creators learn how to **expand beyond traditional content** and step into the world of streaming media… building a platform where **their voice can be seen, heard, and experienced on a larger stage.**

One example is Jay Kay, who is evolving her podcast *Many Wigs* into **The Many Wigs Talk Show**… **turning conversations into a visual show designed for global audiences.**

Because today, authority isn't just about having a message. It's about having a platform.

APPLY NOW

STEP INTO MEDIA MOGUL AND TURN YOUR VOICE INTO A SHOW.

When Enough is Enough

WITH ANGELA DEVANI

"Who have you had to become in order to feel loved?"

This question was asked of me recently and my answer surprised me.

It took me down a rabbit hole of examining my values, my contribution to relationships and in the world, my commitment to myself and my worthiness.

How often do you underestimate your value?
Your Enough-ness?
…And when is Enough, Enough?

For centuries, women have doubted their Enough-ness. We've been abused, beaten, sold, degraded, used and told that we don't matter. I'm not saying that men haven't experienced some of the same treatment, but we know the history of this impact on women has been prevalent.

As I pondered the question "Who have you had to become in order to feel loved?", I reflected on an ex-partner where I felt that I wasn't enough because I no longer worked in a corporate career and was a stay-at-home mom. Some of this feeling was because my ex made comments reflecting his thoughts about me staying home with our young child. Some of this feeling was my own ego.

Additionally, I was in a relationship where I was not told that I was loved and this impacted my ability to feel loved Enough - or at all. His actions may have shown otherwise at times, but those actions were few and the words were said to me about 5 times over 20 years.

I knew I was Enough to my family, friends, community and clients. In fact, I knew that I was More than Enough to them, but that wasn't the same as feeling and knowing I was Enough in the eyes of my husband.

So, I did more to "prove" my value. I gave up who I was to have peace in the home, to please him and to feel Enough.

But it was not Enough.

I didn't think I was Enough, so how could he ever see or know that I was Enough. I had lost that belief in myself.

I had lost my identity.

In the beginning, in his eyes, I was Enough and that's why the relationship worked, but I knew in my heart that he was not Enough for me.

I knew it 3 months into the relationship and I overlooked it.

I ignored my intuition that he would be enough for me because I noticed that he was different than others I had dated.

So, I stayed.

I stayed through the doubt and the criticism.
I stayed through the hurtful words…and lack of loving words.
I stayed for the security I thought I had.

Ultimately, we both sacrificed our values for what we hoped would be Enough, but it wasn't enough to sustain a healthy relationship.

We both decided that there wasn't enough to hold onto.

As I have reclaimed myself over the past 4 years, I have discovered that I was always Enough.

I just had to Remember that.
I had to look deep into my heart and remember my value, my Enough-ness.

I broke the cycles of not being Enough that I discovered in my ancestral lines.
I looked deeply at my identity as a woman, a partner, a mom, a friend, a daughter, a sister, etc….

Each role has its place and what being Enough is.

I Am Enough.
You Are Enough.

How do you Celebrate your Enough-ness?
I hope you will do that today and every day.

Special gift for you

10% off of a 90 minute healing session to heal the past or re-connect to your Enough-ness. Use code "MILLION". Limit 1 per person. Expires 5/31/26.

https://www.elementalmagick.net/service-page/90-minute-private-session

Connect with Angela

https://www.elementalmagick.net

angeladevani1111
https://www.instagram.com/angeladevani1111

Angela Devani
https://www.facebook.com/angeladevani1111

Angela Devani
https://www.linkedin.com/angeladevani1111

THIS NOVEMBER...

The room that *changed everything* is returning

The MILLION DOLLAR Room

A *three-day experience for women* stepping into ***visibility***, ***proximity***, ***power***, and ***expansion.***

NO DISTRACTIONS...

Just the room. The women. The work. The breakthroughs. The visibility.

Your next level... fully activated.

VIP General Admission

- Three full days of transformational sessions
- Keynotes, trainings, activations
- Networking and community
- Access to the Million Dollar Marketplace
- Surprise visibility moments
- First access to apply for speaking opportunities
- Be part of a media production filmed for a movie

Elite VIP Experience

- Three days in the front row
- Welcome Soirée
- VIP only experiences and activations
- VIP Lounge
- Priority access and concierge support
- Exclusive gifts and surprises
- Private VIP only session with special guests

Bigger. Bolder. *More unforgettable than ever.*

GET YOUR TICKETS
FOR NOVEMBER 2026

WITH YOUR HOSTS
NATOSHA, WENDY, & ANISA

Becoming the Liminal Woman

The Practice of Self-Governance in the In-Between Times by Allie Billings

Leaving a monotheistic religion is often described as a simple loss of belief, but that framing doesn't quite capture what is actually happening in the moment someone decides to leave Christianity. What fractures most deeply isn't faith in God or even trust in other people. It's trust in yourself… your sense of self-authority.

For many women, religion functions as an external decision-making algorithm. It tells you what is right and wrong, who you are allowed to be, and what the consequences will be if you step outside those boundaries. When that structure disappears, you are left without a familiar way to answer your questions. **Learning to trust yourself again after that kind of rupture can feel almost impossible.**

I spent years inside a fundamentalist religious system that positioned authority outside of myself and framed personal struggle as personal failure. When truth, morality, and safety are defined externally, it makes sense that your own inner signals begin to feel unreliable or even dangerous.

Part of what makes leaving so destabilising is the realisation that you once believed things that are no longer true for you. That recognition can feel like a betrayal of your own judgement. If I believed that then, how can I trust myself now? The loss of certainty quickly becomes a loss of self-trust, even though your capacity for discernment was never gone. It was simply outsourced to a power structure that rewarded obedience over internal knowing. Our self-betrayal began in those moments when obedience replaced the ability to listen to our own minds and bodies.

This is where the liminal work begins.

Liminality is the state of being in between… when old structures have fallen away and new ones have not yet formed. Identity feels unstable here because it is unstable. That's the point. The self that existed inside religious authority no longer fits, but the self that governs from within hasn't fully come online yet. Many women misread this instability as failure, when it is actually transition.

The nervous system, however, doesn't experience liminality as neutral. It experiences it as threat. Uncertainty registers as danger in the body, and the impulse to resolve it can feel urgent. Many women feel pressure to replace religion immediately with something else… a new belief system, a new ideology, a new certainty. The body wants relief from perceived danger, and religious conditioning often trained decisiveness as safety, pulling us back toward familiar patterns simply to avoid discomfort.

But healing can't happen by rushing to replace one authority with another.

Becoming the liminal woman means learning to stay present in the in-between long enough to hear yourself again over the noise of past conditioning and future expectations. Self-trust is rebuilt through small, ordinary moments of listening.

Try this. When you are hungry before a meal, pause and ask yourself what you actually want. Do I want enchiladas? Notice the response. Do I want a salad? Notice again. There is no right answer. The practice isn't about nutrition or optimisation. **It's about retraining yourself to ask and to listen, even when the response feels unfamiliar.** Religious conditioning can run so deep that even basic internal signals are overridden or moralised. Relearning how to hear yourself may feel uncomfortable, but that discomfort is part of the repair.

This is what the liminal space allows for. It creates room to question without pressure to conclude, to identify values without packaging them into doctrine, and to discover what feels right before declaring it permanent. Over time, this builds something stronger than certainty. It builds confidence in your ability to respond honestly and support yourself through the consequences of your choices.

This stage can't be skipped. When it's rushed, we often find ourselves once again deferring to external authority, mistaking clarity for wisdom and certainty for safety. Liminality is uncomfortable, but it is necessary. It is where autonomy takes root and where ethics become lived and practiced rather than imposed.

To be a liminal woman is not to be lost. It is to be in the process of learning how to stand on your own terms, developing self-governance slowly and deliberately, until your life begins to feel like it is finally being lived from the inside out.

Connect with Allie

Allie | The Liminal Woman
http://tiktok.com/@theliminalwoman/

@the.liminalwoman
http://instagram.com/the.liminalwoman/

JOIN THE PODCAST WAITLIST

https://alexandra-billings.mykajabi.com/the-liminal-woman-podcast-waitlist

WANT TO **GET PUBLISHED** IN MILLION DOLLAR MOM INC MAGAZINE?

Million Dollar Mom Inc. Magazine is not just a publication. It is a **premium visibility platform created for ambitious women** who understand that influence is built intentionally.

Distributed digitally and in print through Amazon and IngramSpark, Million Dollar Mom Inc. Magazine **offers global accessibility** while maintaining a **luxury**, **high-level brand standard**. Contributors also benefit from **expanded visibility through our email marketing, social platforms, community ecosystem,** and **media network.**

Visit the website to learn more & apply to be published.

CLICK HERE

YOUR PUBLISHING OPTIONS:

PUBLISH AN ARTICLE	STRATEGIC AD PLACEMENT	BACK COVER FEATURE	FRONT COVER FEATURE
Thought leadership article, up to 600 word count	Place your brand inside a magazine aligned with leadership, influence, and impact.	Includes a high-impact four-page spread designed to showcase your brand with intention and authority.	The most premium placement, including a six-page spread and front-of-magazine visibility that sets the tone for the entire issue.
FREE	$97	$497	$997

When Soundbites Weren't Enough

The Birth and Vision of WSOS: Scripture Over Soundbites with Kelly Parker

In a digital world saturated with bite-sized wisdom, viral affirmations, and endlessly recycled talking points...

Kelly Parker felt a growing tension she could no longer ignore. Everywhere she looked, truth was being reduced to slogans. Discernment was being replaced with popularity. And faith, once a grounding force, was being reshaped into something more palatable, more convenient, and often more self-focused.

That tension became the seed of WSOS: Scripture Over Soundbites.

The podcast was not born out of a marketing strategy or a trend forecast. It emerged from a quiet but persistent sense that something essential was being lost in modern conversations, especially those aimed at women seeking growth, leadership, and purpose. Kelly, a business coach, speaker, and founder of the Make Your Mark Movement™, had spent years working with women navigating transitions: leaving direct sales, rebuilding identity, disentangling belief systems, and learning how to lead without losing themselves.

Again and again, she noticed a pattern. Many women were consuming vast amounts of content but felt more confused, not clearer. More empowered on the surface, yet more anxious underneath. They were told to trust themselves above all else, to manifest outcomes, to speak their truth, yet were often left without an anchor when life pushed back. Kelly didn't see this as a failure of effort or intelligence. She saw it as a misalignment of foundations.

"Scripture had quietly moved from being the source to being the accessory," she observed. "Something people referenced occasionally instead of something that formed them deeply."

A DISTRESS SIGNAL, NOT A PLATFORM

The name WSOS was intentional. In aviation and maritime history, SOS has always been a signal; a call for help, clarity, rescue, or recalibration. By adding the "W," Kelly reframed it as a cultural signal rather than a personal crisis: We need Scripture over soundbites.

The podcast was designed as a response to a moment in time, not just a personal project. Kelly saw a widening gap between what culture celebrates and what Scripture actually teaches and she believed women were being caught in the middle. Not because they lacked faith, but because they were being discipled by algorithms more than by wisdom.

The early episodes set the tone immediately. This would not be a podcast built on outrage or performative hot takes. It would not chase trends or echo what was already loud. Instead, WSOS would slow the conversation down. It would examine popular narratives around self-worth, ambition, femininity, leadership, suffering, and success through the lens of Scripture, lived experience, and spiritual discernment.

Kelly approached each episode with the posture of a guide, not a guru. She wasn't interested in telling women what to think, but in helping them see clearly enough to decide wisely.

FROM BUSINESS COACHING TO CULTURAL DISCERNMENT

Although WSOS is faith-centered, its roots are deeply connected to Kelly's professional journey. Years of working with women through business revealed that mindset struggles were rarely about confidence alone. They were about belief systems often inherited, absorbed, or subtly distorted over time.

Women would say they felt "off," "stuck," or "lost," even when they were doing all the "right" things. Kelly began to recognize that many weren't lost at all. They were misaligned, trying to build lives and businesses on narratives that didn't match their values or convictions.
That realization became the foundation for one of the podcast's core themes: alignment over achievement.

WSOS explores how cultural soundbites; phrases like "protect your peace at all costs" or "you owe no one anything", can sound empowering while quietly eroding responsibility, humility, and community. Kelly doesn't dismiss the desire for boundaries or rest; instead, she asks better questions. What happens when self-preservation becomes the highest value? What do we lose when discomfort is treated as danger? How does Scripture invite strength without self-worship? These questions resonate far beyond the podcast microphone.

A DIFFERENT KIND OF AUTHORITY

One of the most distinctive aspects of WSOS is its tone. Kelly intentionally avoids the performance-driven confidence that dominates much online content. Instead, she models authority rooted in humility; speaking from experience, Scripture, and reflection rather than certainty for certainty's sake.

Listeners quickly recognize that this is not a podcast about perfection. It's about formation.

Kelly often speaks to the unseen costs of cultural narratives: the children watching their parents, the marriages strained by hyper-individualism, the friendships weakened when self-interest eclipses loyalty. She challenges the idea that strength must look aggressive, that leadership requires dominance, or that being "unbothered" is the goal.

In doing so, WSOS creates space for women who feel out of step with modern extremes but haven't had language for why.

THE VISION BEYOND THE MICROPHONE

While the podcast is the most visible expression of WSOS, Kelly is clear that it is only the beginning. Her long-term vision extends far beyond weekly episodes.

She sees WSOS as a foundation for deeper discipleship, thoughtful dialogue, and community formation, particularly for women navigating leadership, business, and influence without wanting to compromise their faith. Future expansions include guided resources, long-form teachings, live conversations, and curated spaces where women can process cultural messages together rather than in isolation.

At its core, the vision is simple but countercultural: to help women move from reaction to discernment, from consumption to contemplation, from noise to truth.

Kelly is not interested in building a following that merely agrees with her. She hopes to cultivate listeners who think critically, pray deeply, and live courageously, even when that means standing apart.

A RETURN TO ROOTS

In many ways, WSOS: Scripture Over Soundbites represents a return rather than a reinvention. It calls women back to the kind of wisdom that doesn't need to be viral to be valid. Back to Scripture not as a quote bank, but as a formative guide. Back to leadership that blends strength with surrender.

As the podcast continues to grow, Kelly remains anchored to the same conviction that sparked its creation: when foundations are clear, direction follows.

In a world racing toward louder opinions and faster answers, WSOS offers something rare; a space to listen, discern, and realign. And for the women tuning in, that may be the most powerful signal of all.

Connect with Kelly

- https://kellyparkerxo.com/start-here
- passiontoprofitplan
  https://www.instagram.com/passiontoprofitplan
- Kelly Parker
  https://facebook.com/kellypassionandpurpose
- Christian Women Influencers & Leaders Group
  https://facebook.com/groups/christianwomeninfluencersandleaders
- WSOS: Scripture over Soundbites Podcast
  https://podcasts.apple.com/us/podcast/wsos-scripture-over-soundbites/id1866710955

Gifts for you

- Unscriptured: Reclaiming Your Voice, Your Vision, and Your Worth Through God's Truth
- Break Free: 3 Simple Shifts to Move Past Limiting Beliefs

www.ingramcontent.com/pod-product-compliance
Lightning Source LLC
LaVergne TN
LVRC080248220926
848482LV00042B/350

* 9 7 9 8 9 9 5 2 1 6 6 0 5 *